DOUG MIENTKIEWICZ

JIM KAAT

KIRBY PUCKETT

CHUCK KNOBLAUCH

TONY OLIVA

BERT BLYLEVEN

KENT HRBEK

CHRISTIAN GUZMAN

ROD CAREW

BRAD RADKE

GARY GAETTI

HARMON KILLEBREW

THE HISTORY OF THE
MINNESOTA
TWINS

AARON FRISCH

CREATIVE ⚫ EDUCATION

Published by Creative Education, 123 South Broad Street, Mankato, MN 56001

Creative Education is an imprint of The Creative Company.

Designed by Rita Marshall.

Photographs by AllSport (Jonathan Daniel, Tom Pigeon, Rick Stewart, Matthew Stockman),

Associated Press/Wide World Photos, FotoSport (Mitch Reibel), Icon Sports Media (David Seelig),

Diane Johnson, SportsChrome (Louis Raynor, Rob Tringali Jr., Steve Woltman)

Library of Congress Cataloging-in-Publication Data

Frisch, Aaron. The history of the Minnesota Twins / by Aaron Frisch.

p. cm. — (Baseball)   ISBN 1-58341-214-X

Summary: Highlights the key personalities and memorable games in the history of the

Minnesota Twins, a team that moved from Washington, D.C., to the Twin Cities area in 1961.

1. Minnesota Twins (Baseball team)—History—

Juvenile literature. I. Title. II. Baseball (Mankato, Minn.).

GV875.M55 F75 2002   796.357'64'09776569—dc21   2001047873

First Edition 9 8 7 6 5 4 3 2 1

MINNEAPOLIS

AND ST. PAUL, SEPARATED BY THE MIGHTY MISSISSIPPI

River, are the two largest cities in Minnesota. Minneapolis is the more modern of the two and features an impressive glass-and-metal skyline, while St. Paul is the state's capital and is characterized by its historic brick buildings. Together, the Twin Cities are home to much **5** of the state's population.

Long winters inspire people in the Twin Cities and throughout the state to live life to the fullest once the ice and snow drifts finally melt away. With its great forests and thousands of lakes, Minnesota offers abundant opportunities for anglers, campers, and other outdoor enthusiasts. Since 1961, Minnesota summers have also included major league baseball. That year, a struggling team from

ZOILO VERSALLES

the East Coast found a new home in the Twin Cities. Naturally, the team was named the Twins.

In **1962**, lefty Jack Kralick pitched Minnesota's first no-hitter, blanking the Kansas City A's.

{THE TWINS BEGIN} The Twins started out in Washington, D.C., where the franchise was known as the Senators. Founded in 1901, the Senators won the 1924 World Series but steadily declined after that. Fan attendance gradually dropped off as the losses piled up, and in 1961, team owner Calvin Griffith announced that the team was moving to the Twin Cities, where it would get a new start as the Minnesota Twins.

The Twins featured several fine young players during their early years. The first of these budding stars was a stocky, muscular slugger named Harmon Killebrew. Although Killebrew was a solid defender in either the infield or outfield, he was best known for his towering home run blasts. From 1962 to 1964, "the Killer" led

TORII HUNTER

Outfielder Tony Oliva made the AL All-Star team every season from **1964** to **1971**.

TONY OLIVA

the American League (AL) in home runs every season.

But Killebrew wasn't Minnesota's only fine hitter. Right fielder

Tony Oliva had a sweet swing that allowed him to

smack pitches to any part of the field. As a rookie in

1964, he batted .323 and won the AL batting title. But

even Killebrew and Oliva were overshadowed in 1965

by shortstop Zoilo Versalles. Known for his blazing

speed, Versalles scored 126 runs and was named the AL's Most

Valuable Player (MVP).

Behind the efforts of their great trio, the Twins roared up the

standings with a 102–60 record in 1965 and won the AL pennant. In

the World Series, the Twins battled to a draw with the Los Angeles

Dodgers after six games. In the deciding game seven, however,

Minnesota couldn't hit Dodgers ace Sandy Koufax, losing the game

and the championship 2–0.

Outfielder Bob Allison made Twins history in **1963** by jacking three home runs in one game.

BOB ALLISON

Like the great
Rod Carew,
Chuck
Knoblauch
was a Twins
standout at
second base.

CHUCK KNOBLAUCH

{MOVING UP IN MINNESOTA} Despite the heartbreaking

loss, Minnesota fans were confident that the Twins would get another

Hurler Jim Kaat won 25 games during the **1966** season, setting a club record that still stands.

shot at the title. Besides Killebrew, Oliva, and

Versalles, Minnesota featured such fine fielders as

catcher Earl Battey and outfielder Bob Allison. The

pitching staff, meanwhile, included such talented

hurlers as Jim "Mudcat" Grant, Jim Perry, Dean

12   Chance, and Jim Kaat.

The Twins bolstered their lineup even further in 1967 with the

addition of rookie second baseman Rod Carew. With a sharp eye

and superb bat control, Carew became an instant star, slapping hit

after hit en route to the AL Rookie of the Year award. "Rod Carew

could get more hits with a soup bone than I could get with a rack

full of bats," said Twins outfielder Steve Brye.

In 1969, Killebrew slammed 49 home runs and drove in

ROD CAREW

140 runs to win the AL MVP award. Behind Carew and the Killer,

Minnesota claimed the AL Western Division crown (the AL was

divided into two divisions in 1969). The Twins then advanced to the

AL Championship Series (ALCS), where they fell to the powerful

Baltimore Orioles in three straight games.

The next year was a replay of the same story. Minnesota won its division and reached the ALCS to face Baltimore. Once again, the

Orioles dispatched the Twins and went on to win the World Series.

One **1972**
game between
Minnesota and
Milwaukee
went 22
innings and
lasted nearly
six hours.
"We had some great ballclubs back then," Killebrew

later said. "But Baltimore always had our number."

Unfortunately, 17 seasons would pass before the

Twins would again reach the postseason. Knee injuries

soon took their toll on Oliva, and other stars such as

Killebrew and Perry retired. Even though Carew and pitcher Bert

Blyleven gave Minnesota some great performances throughout the

mid-1970s, the Twins' glory years slipped further and further

behind them.

{**"HERBIE" AND KIRBY**} In the late 1970s, Twins owner

Calvin Griffith began to trade away most of the team's high-paid

veterans and replace them with young, inexpensive players. By 1981,

as the Twins celebrated their 20th season in Minnesota, they were

BRAD RADKE

in trouble. The Twins finished dead last in their division that year,

and attendance at Metropolitan Stadium reached new lows.

Just when it looked like the Twins would never recover, they

made several great moves. In 1981, the team added a hard-hitting

young first baseman named Kent Hrbek to the lineup. Then, in 1982,

the team moved into the Hubert H. Humphrey Metrodome—a new

indoor stadium with a fiberglass roof—in downtown Minneapolis

and selected a stocky outfielder named Kirby Puckett in the 1982

amateur draft.

The 5-foot-9 and 220-pound Puckett joined the

Twins' starting lineup in 1984, and his nonstop hustle

and ever-present smile quickly endeared him to

Minnesota fans. Of course, it didn't hurt that he was

also a dynamo on the field, patrolling center field with his sure

glove and hitting scorching line drives. "Scouts would always tell me

I was too short, or too heavy, or too whatever," Puckett said. "But

baseball isn't about being a shape or a size. It's about how big you

are inside that counts."

With "Herbie" and Kirby leading the way, the Twins inched

their way back up the standings. By 1986, Minnesota had the

makings of a powerful offense. Hrbek, Puckett, third baseman

Kent Hrbek hit a 12th-inning, game-winning home run in his first big-league game (in **1982**).

KENT HRBEK

With players such as third baseman Kone Koskie, the Twins are known for their hustle.

Gary Gaetti, and right fielder Tom Brunansky could all knock the

cover off the ball. Unfortunately, the team's pitching was weak, and

the Twins sank back into last place.

{T.K. AND THE AMAZING TWINS} In 1987, the

Twins brought in Tom Kelly as their new manager. At

36 years old, the low-key Kelly became the youngest

skipper in the major leagues. Under his guidance,

the Twins' pitching improved immediately. Left-handed starter

Frank "Sweet Music" Viola and veteran Bert Blyleven combined for

32 wins that season, and closer Jeff Reardon racked up 31 saves.

Meanwhile, Minnesota's power hitters—Hrbek, Puckett,

Gaetti, and Brunansky—each hit at least 28 homers as the

surprising Twins topped the AL West with an 85–77 record. "We

just do what T.K. [Kelly] tells us," Puckett explained. "Don't get too

high or too low. Just go out, give 100 percent, and we'll win the

KIRBY PUCKETT

battle one game at a time."

But Minnesota wasn't content with just a division crown.

In the ALCS, the Twins toppled the favored Detroit Tigers four

games to one. For the first time in 22 years, the Twins were back

in the World Series. The Twins were an underdog again, facing the

powerful St. Louis Cardinals, but playing in front of a raucous

Metrodome crowd, the Twins crushed the Cardinals 10–1 and

8–4 in the first two games.

St. Louis then won the next three games at home,

taking a 3–2 series lead back to the Dome. But

Minnesota won game six and refused to let game

seven slip away. Viola took the mound in the

deciding game and surrendered only six hits as the

Twins won 4–2. Minnesota was a world champion at last!

By 1990, however, the Twins had stumbled back to last place.

Blyleven and Viola had been traded away, and the team struggled as

its young pitchers learned the ropes. "We just aren't getting it done

on the mound," Kelly said. "But hopefully the lumps we take now

will pay off down the road."

{THE GREATEST WORLD SERIES EVER} Minnesota sputtered

early in 1991 but finished atop the division with a 95–67 mark

FRANK VIOLA

A fan favorite, tough third baseman Gary Gaetti spent 10 seasons in Minnesota.

GARY GAETTI

thanks to a late-season surge. The team's momentum carried over into the ALCS, where the Twins trounced the Toronto Blue Jays in five games. Unbelievably, Minnesota was back in the World Series.

Facing the Twins were the Atlanta Braves, a team that had also finished in last place in its division the previous season. Atlanta had a lot of young talent, but Minnesota was loaded as well. The rebuilt pitching staff included starters Scott Erickson, Kevin Tapani, veteran Jack Morris, and closer Rick Aguilera. Other key additions included slugging designated hitter Chili Davis and rookie second baseman Chuck Knoblauch.

The series was an epic battle, going seven nail-biting games. As had happened in 1987, Minnesota won the first two games at the Metrodome before losing three straight on the road. With the Twins on the ropes, Puckett dominated game six. After making a

In **1991**, Scott Erickson won 12 straight starts to help the Twins capture another AL pennant.

SCOTT ERICKSON

spectacular, run-saving catch in the third inning, Puckett strode to

the plate in the 11th inning and crushed a pitch into the left-field

stands to win the game and extend the series.

Game seven pitted Morris against Braves ace John Smoltz.

Each was outstanding, and the game remained scoreless after nine

innings. Kelly told Morris he intended to bring in a reliever in the 10th, but the fiery veteran insisted on returning to the mound. "I would have needed a shotgun to get him out of the game," said Kelly. "And I didn't have one."

Morris needed to pitch only one more inning. In the bottom of the 10th, Twins pinch hitter Gene Larkin looped a hit into left field that scored outfielder Dan Gladden from third base. The Metrodome crowd let loose a deafening roar as Gladden jumped on home plate to give the Twins their second world title. Fay Vincent, the commissioner of baseball, said it best when he proclaimed, "It was probably the greatest World Series ever."

{A DIFFICULT DECADE} Minnesota's standing atop the baseball world did not last, however. The Twins went 90–72 in 1992 but missed the postseason. Then, in the years that followed, Minnesota slipped from contention. Owner Carl Pohlad refused to

Left fielder Dan Gladden smacked a pair of doubles and triples in the **1991** World Series.

DAN GLADDEN

pay big salaries to bring in established stars, and the Twins struggled

as they tried to develop new talent.

Marty Cordova
won **1995**
AL Rookie of
the Year
honors with
24 homers
and 20
stolen bases.

Young players such as outfielder Marty Cordova

and pitcher Brad Radke played well, but the losses

piled up. Then, before the 1996 season, the Twins were

dealt a crushing blow; Puckett developed blurred vision

in his right eye—a disease called glaucoma—and was

forced to retire.

In the mid-1990s, the team was led by several veterans who

returned to spend their final seasons in their native state of

Minnesota. These included infielder Paul Molitor, designated hitter

Dave Winfield, and catcher Terry Steinbach—all former All-Stars.

The Twins continued to post losing records, but Steinbach saw a key

reason for optimism: Tom Kelly's coaching skills. "He concentrates

on playing the game right," Steinbach said. "His players run balls

MARTY CORDOVA

out. They hit the cutoff man. They don't showboat or hot dog."

There remained little to showboat about in the late 1990s as the Twins remained in the division cellar. In 1998, Chuck Knoblauch, the team's top player, asked to be traded and was sent to the New York Yankees. Pohlad then slashed the Twins' payroll to a league-low $15 million, leaving the team with a lineup full of rookies.

Infielder Todd Walker tied a Minnesota record with base hits in nine straight at-bats in **1998**.

{FORTY YEARS AND COUNTING} By 2000, the Twins'

future looked bleak. The team had suffered eight straight losing seasons, and few experts saw much hope for the future. But in 2001, things suddenly began looking up. First, Puckett and Winfield were inducted into Baseball's Hall of Fame. Then, despite their tiny payroll, the Twins began to win again.

Years of struggling and player development finally paid off as the scrappy Twins led the AL Central Division for much of the

TODD WALKER

Perhaps the fastest player in baseball, Christian Guzman ripped 20 triples in **2000**.

CHRISTIAN GUZMAN

In **2001**, defensive marvel Doug Mientkiewicz earned his first Gold Glove award.

DOUG MIENTKIEWICZ

season and finished with an 85–77 record. The team featured an

impressive pitching staff led by Brad Radke and Eric Milton,

and opponents found few weaknesses in the Twins'

defense, which included such rising stars as acrobatic

center fielder Torii Hunter, speedy shortstop Christian

Guzman, and first baseman Doug Mientkiewicz.

For more than 40 years, the Twins have been

adding to the fun of Minnesota summers. During those years, the

team has featured some of baseball's all-time greats and won two

world championships. Now, after struggling for the better part of

a decade, the Twins are determined to add to their title total in the

21st century.

Fans hoped that starting pitcher Joe Mays would help the Twins fly high in **2003** and beyond.

JOE MAYS